Healthy Body Image

by Martha E. H. Rustad

PEBBLE
a capstone imprint

Pebble Explore is published by Pebble, an imprint of Capstone
1710 Roe Crest Drive
North Mankato, Minnesota 56003
www.capstonepub.com

Library of Congress Cataloging-in-Publication Data
Names: Rustad, Martha E. H. (Martha Elizabeth Hillman), 1975- author.
Title: Healthy body image / Martha E. H. Rustad.
Description: North Mankato : Capstone Press, 2021. | Series: Health and my body | Includes bibliographical references and index. | Audience: Ages 6-8 | Audience: Grades 2-3 | Summary: "Tall. Short. Big. Small. Bodies come in all shapes and sizes. They change as you get older. Making healthy choices, exercising, and getting enough sleep will help you be the best version of yourself. You only have one body, and it's important to love the one you have"— Provided by publisher.
Identifiers: LCCN 2020025203 (print) | LCCN 2020025204 (ebook) | ISBN 9781977132185 (library binding) | ISBN 9781977133205 (trade paperback) | ISBN 9781977154323 (pdf)
Subjects: LCSH: Body image in children—Juvenile literature. | Self-acceptance—Juvenile literature.
Classification: LCC BF723.B6 R87 2021 (print) | LCC BF723.B6 (ebook) | DDC 306.4/613—dc23
LC record available at https://lccn.loc.gov/2020025203
LC ebook record available at https://lccn.loc.gov/2020025204

Image Credits
iStockphoto: FatCamera, 5, 14, 21, 22; pixelfusion3d, 24; Shutterstock: AnnaStills, 25; CREATISTA, 19; Din Mohd Yaman, 16; Dragon Images, 11; Elena Sherengovskaya, 7; girl-think-position, 6; Lordn, 27; mimagephotography, 29; Monkey Business Images, cover; Natee K Jindakum, 18; photonova, design element throughout; Rawpixel.com, 8; Supavadee butradee, 13; WitthayaP, 4

Editorial Credits
Editor: Christianne Jones; Designer: Sarah Bennett; Media Researcher: Morgan Walters; Production Specialist: Laura Manthe

Printed and bound in the United States of America. PO3837

Table of Contents

Bold words are in the glossary.

Healthy Body Image

Everyone is different. Everyone's body is **unique**. It is healthy to have a good **body image**. Your body image is the way you feel about how you look.

Think of how many things you can
do with your body. You can hang from
the monkey bars. You can jump over
a puddle. You can smell yummy food.
You can hear a friend laugh.

Think about what you like about your body. Do you like your strong arms? Do you like the color of your eyes? Do you like your big smile? There are so many things to love about your body!

Is your hair curly or straight? Is it light or dark? Is it long or short? No matter what it is, it is unique to you! There is only one you in the world. Celebrate yourself!

Every single body is different. There isn't a right or wrong body shape. There isn't one perfect body shape.

Some people are tall. Other people are short. People have different skin colors. All colors are beautiful. Everyone has hair that looks different.

We know everyone looks unique. That is what makes the world so interesting. We are thankful for everyone and their differences.

Your Growing Body

We all grow and change in our own ways. You might change from one birthday to the next. Maybe your pants are too short. You got taller! It might be that your shirt is too small. You grew bigger.

Maybe you are still the same size. That is OK too. You will grow when your body is ready. Everyone grows and changes at different times.

It can be hard to be patient while you are waiting to grow. During this time, take good care of your body.

Eat good food. Your body needs **vitamins** and **minerals** to grow healthy and strong. Choose healthy fruits and vegetables for snacks. A banana with peanut butter is yummy. So are carrots dipped in hummus or a colorful salad.

Drink lots of water. Your body needs water to work well. Fill up a water bottle at the beginning of the day. Refill it as needed all day long.

Exercise helps your muscles grow strong. Be active every day. Play hard for at least an hour. Go for a bike ride. Go swimming. Play tag with friends. Jump rope. Just keep moving!

Your heart and lungs need to work hard each day. Being active will help them stay healthy.

Keep your body clean. Wash your hair and body a few times each week. You will smell fresh and clean.

A child's body needs about ten hours of sleep each night. As you sleep, your body recovers from the day. It makes tiny things called **proteins**. You need proteins to stay well and grow.

If you don't get enough sleep, your body can't make these proteins. It is OK to get less sleep once in a while. Your body can catch up from a few nights of bad sleep. But try to stick to a set bedtime **routine**. Then your body will stay healthy and grow.

Self-Esteem

Self-esteem means that you believe in yourself. It is part of having a healthy body image. You can build up your own self-esteem.

Be brave. Try something new. If you don't do it perfectly the first time, try again. Don't give up! Feel proud when you do a little better each time you try. Tell yourself, "Good job!" Believe in yourself. Your self-esteem will grow.

Everyone has a **talent** to share. Finding your special talent might take some work. You might have to try lots of different things. Focus on what you can do well.

Some kids are good at sports. If you like to play sports, join a team. Your school may have sports teams. Some towns have teams for kids too.

Kids on teams help each other. They work together. They cheer each other on! Being on a team helps build up your self-esteem.

Some kids like music. Learning music is good for your brain. Music is also a good way to share your feelings.

If you like to sing, you could join a choir. You could also take singing lessons. You could even write your own song!

You could learn to play an instrument. Maybe you want to try to play piano. Maybe you want to try to play the guitar. You could try different kinds of instruments and see what you like best.

Some kids love stories. If you like to tell stories, write them down. All you need is a pencil and paper. You could ask friends to act out your stories.

Some kids are artists. They can draw. They can paint. Others like to make things with clay. Some build models of cars or other vehicles.

Stories and art make the world beautiful. They can help people relax and feel good.

Spend time doing what you like. This helps you feel good about yourself. Then your self-esteem will grow. Challenge yourself to try something new, even if you are scared. You might be surprised at what you can do!

Everyone has different talents. Keep working on yours. And keep finding new ones. The world would be boring if everyone had the same skills. Share your unique talents with the world!

Helping Others

You can help people around you have a healthy body image too. Tell people what you like about them. Give someone a **compliment**. It will help them feel good. And you will feel good too!

Having a good body image is healthy. Accept your body. It is great just the way it is. Love your body. It can do so many amazing things. Take care of your body. It's the only one you will get!

Glossary

body image (BAH-dee IM-ij)—the way you feel about your body

compliment (KAHM-pluh-muhnt)—praising someone about something

mineral (MIN-ur-uhl)—a part of food that helps keep people healthy

protein (PROH-teen)—the thing found in all living plant and animal cells

routine (roo-TEEN)—a set of actions that become a habit

self-esteem (SELF ess-TEEM)—the way you feel about yourself

talent (TAL-uhnt)—a natural ability or skill

unique (yoo-NEEK)—one of a kind

vitamin (VYE-tuh-min)—a part of food that helps keep people healthy

Read More

Bushman, Susanne M. *Create Positive Habits.* Minneapolis: Jump!, Inc, 2020.

Harris, Robie H. *Who We Are!: All About Being the Same and Being Different.* Somerville, MA: Candlewick Press, 2016.

Heneghan, Judith. *All Kinds of Bodies.* New York: Crabtree, 2020.

Internet Sites

Body Image and Self-Esteem
kidshealth.org/en/teens/body-image.html

How Can I Feel Better About My Body?
www.kidshealth.org/en/kids/feel-better-about-body.html

My Plate Kids' Place
www.choosemyplate.gov/browse-by-audience/view-all-audiences/children/kids

Index